GREEKS AND PERSIANS GO TO WAR

WAR BOOK BEST SELLERS

Children's Ancient History

BABY PROFESSOR

EDUCATION KIDS

Speedy Publishing LLC
40 E. Main St. #1156
Newark, DE 19711
www.speedypublishing.com
Copyright 2017

It looked like a one-sided fight. Persia was much larger than Greece, had a bigger army, and was richer. The Greeks often fought each other as much as they fought external enemies. Yet Greece won the Persian Wars. How did they do that? Let's find out.

FIFTY YEARS OF WAR

Persia was a huge empire centered on what is now Iran. Greece was not a single nation, but a large collection of city-states. The Greek world extended far beyond what we see on a map today: Greek colonies flourished as far west as Spain, along the shores of the Black Sea, and along the coast of what is now Turkey.

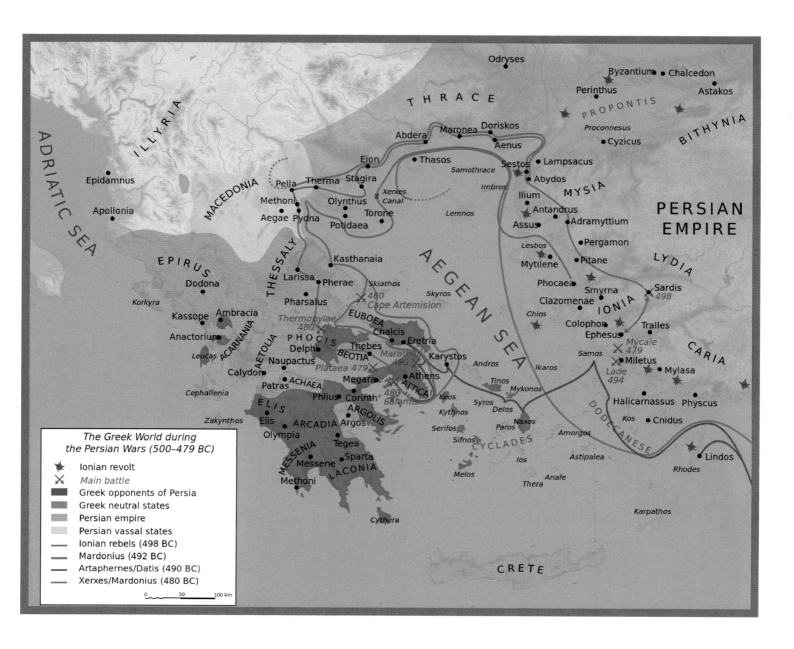

The Greek World during the Persian Wars (500–479 BC)

★ Ionian revolt
✕ Main battle
Greek opponents of Persia
Greek neutral states
Persian empire
Persian vassal states
— Ionian rebels (498 BC)
— Mardonius (492 BC)
— Artaphernes/Datis (490 BC)
— Xerxes/Mardonius (480 BC)

0   50   100 km

ADRIATIC SEA

ILLYRIA

THRACE

Odryses

Byzantium • Chalcedon
Perinthus
PROPONTIS
Astakos
BITHYNIA
Proconnesus
Cyzicus

Abdera Maronea Doriskos
Aenus
Eion Thasos Sestos Lampsacus
Therma Stagira Samothrace Abydos
Pella Xerxes Imbros Ilium MYSIA
Methoni Canal Antandrus
Olynthus Adramyttium
Aegae Pydna Torone Lemnos Assus
Potidaea Pergamon
Lesbos Pitane
Mytilene
Phocaea Smyrna Sardis
Clazomenae 498
Chios IONIA
Colophon Tralles
Ephesus
Mycale Samos 479
Lade Miletus Mylasa
494

PERSIAN
EMPIRE

LYDIA

CARIA

Epidamnus

Apollonia

MACEDONIA

EPIRUS
Dodona
Korkyra
Kassope Ambracia
Anactorium ACARNANIA
Leucas AETOLIA
Calydon
Naupactus
Patras ACHAEA
Phlius
Corinth
ELIS ARGOLIS
Elis ARCADIA Argos
Olympia Tegea
MESSENIA Sparta
Messene LACONIA
Methoni
Cythera

THESSALY
Larissa Pherae
Pharsalus
Kasthanaia
Skiathos
480 Cape Artemision
Thermopylae
480 EUBOEA
PHOCIS Chalcis
Delphi Thebes Eretria
BEOTIA
Plataea 479 Marathon
Megara 490 Karystos
ATTICA
Athens
480
Salamis

AEGEAN SEA

Skyros

Andros
Ikaros
Keos Tinos Mykonos
Kythnos Syros Delos
Serifos Paros Naxos
Sifnos Ios Amorgos
Melos CYCLADES Astipalea
Thera Anafe

Zakynthos
Cephallenia

Halicarnassus Physcus
DODECANESE
Kos Cnidus
Rhodes
Lindos

Karpathos

CRETE

Anatolia

Troesmis
AD.
ae
Tomis
LOWER
29
MOE
A.D.
ACE
Apollonia
Adrianopolis
Byzantium
Constantinople
Calchedon
Nicomedia
BITHYNIA
74

Heraclea
KINGDOM OF THE
CIMMERIAN BOSPORUS

BLACK SEA

Sinope
PAPHLAGONIA
64
Gangra
Amasia
PONTUS
Zela 63 A.D.
Nicopolis

Dioscur
Zichi
Sebast
Trapez

LESSER ARME

Heraclea
Ancyra
GALATIA
25
KINGDOM OF
DEIOTARUS
7
Halys R.
Caesarea
Melitene

Eup

MYSIA
Pergamum
133
ASIA
Sardis
LYDIA

PHRYGIA
103
148
Iconium
LYCAONIA
25
CAPPADOCIA
18 A.D.
Samosata

COMMA-
GENE

OSR

PISIDIA
25
PAMPHYLIA
102
CILICIA
67
Anthemusias
64
Apamea

Miletus
CARIA
LYCIA
43 A.D.
102

Antioch
COELES

Rhodes

Salamis
Emesa

Carpathus

CYPRUS

FENICIA
SYRIA

As Persia expanded west into Anatolia (now Turkey), it encountered and started to conquer Greek city-states. The whole Greek world had to try to unite to face this threat.

The fighting took place off and on for about fifty years, from 500 to 449 BCE. Despite great challenges, the Greeks were able to win.

Spruner Map of Greece, Epirus after the Persian War

THE GROWTH OF PERSIA

Once Persia conquered Lydia, in what is now Turkey, it held a large amount of territory and power on the edge of the Greek world. The Persians began attacking and conquering the Greek city-states along the Mediterranean coast.

In 500 BCE the conquered city-states rebelled against the empire. The rebellion lasted six years and failed. At one point Athens and its allies sent a fleet to support the rebellion. Darius, the Persian emperor, decided he should conquer mainland Greece to get rid of this threat on his border. The first attempt to invade Greece, in 492, involved a huge army and fleet. But many ships were sunk in a sudden storm, Darius called off the invasion.

Darius III of Persia

Plain of Marathon

MARATHON

In 490 the Persians were back! They took control of Thrace and Macedonia in the north of Greece. Then they landed an army of more than 25,000 men on the Plain of Marathon, about 25 miles from Athens.

Supporting forces from Sparta did not arrive in time, and the Athenians faced the invaders with just 10,000 men. Noticing that the Persian cavalry was not around, the Greeks launched an attack and won a huge victory, killing over 6,000 Persian soldiers while losing fewer than 200 themselves. It was the first major victory by the Greeks over the Persians, and the Persian army abandoned their invasion.

Persian Army

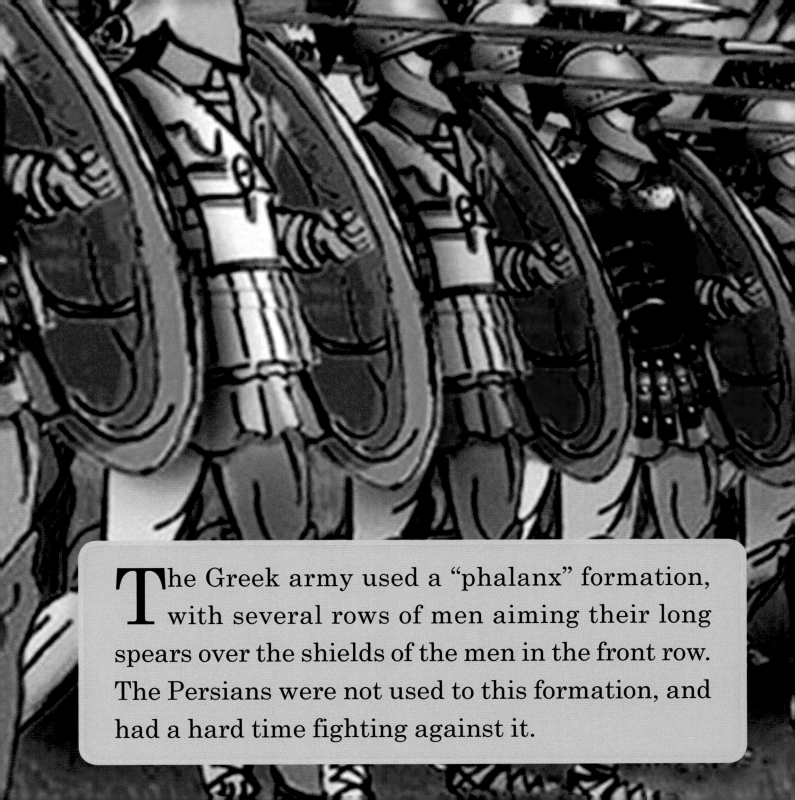

The Greek army used a "phalanx" formation, with several rows of men aiming their long spears over the shields of the men in the front row. The Persians were not used to this formation, and had a hard time fighting against it.

Phalanx

The victory at Marathon stopped the Persian advance, although they had gained territory. The victory gave new confidence to the Greeks, and in Athens it ushered in a "golden age" of innovation, political advances, and creativity.

Plain of Marathon

King Xerxes and his Army

THERMOPYLAE

In 480 the Persians, under King Xerxes, invaded again. Their army was so large that it moved very slowly, and this time many Greek city-states had time to organize a common defense. Sparta was in charge of the army and Athens was in charge of the navy.

Hugely outnumbered, the Greeks decided to fight at Thermopylae, holding a narrow pass which they could defend with a much smaller number of men. Only a small part of the Persian army could attack at any time. At the same time the Persian fleet tried to attack, but a huge storm sank many ships while the Greek ships waited in harbors until the storm was over.

Thermopylae

Phocis

The Persians attacked at Thermopylae for two days with no success, and suffered heavy losses, with tens of thousands of Persian soldiers wounded or killed. But then a Greek traitor showed the Persians a path around the pass so they could attack the Greeks from two sides. The Greeks had put one thousand men from Phocis to guard that path, but they heard a rumor that their city was being attacked and rushed home to defend it. The rumor was untrue.

Seeing that the Greek position was lost, the Spartan commander sent away most of the army so it could fight again. Then 300 Spartans, with one thousand soldiers from Thespis and 400 from Thebes, continued to hold off the Persians, killing many of the enemy, until they were wiped out.

Thebes

Spartan

HISTORY AND MOVIES

This battle is the subject of a popular 2007 movie, "300". That movie implies that only the Spartans were left to hold off the Persian onslaught, which makes for a great movie but is not what actually happened.

The movie is inaccurate in another way. It shows the Greeks as honest and heroic while the Persians are nasty and cruel. But the Persian nation was much more complicated than the evil kingdom in a movie. Its founder, Cyrus the Great, was the first ruler in the whole world (that we know of) to declare that everyone in the kingdom had basic rights and freedoms. On the other side, although the Greeks were the founders of democracy and

 philosophy, they were slave-owners and could be cruel to their enemies—and even sometimes their allies.

Tomb of Cyrus the Great

AFTER THE BATTLE

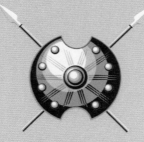

Hearing that their land forces had lost the battle, the Greek navy ended a sea battle with the Persians and withdrew. So the Persians had won the day! But you can win a battle and lose a war, as the Phoenicians soon found out.

SALAMIS

The Persians continued to advance. Their armies captured and burned Greek cities, and their fleet attempted to destroy the Greek fleet.

Salamis

Triremes

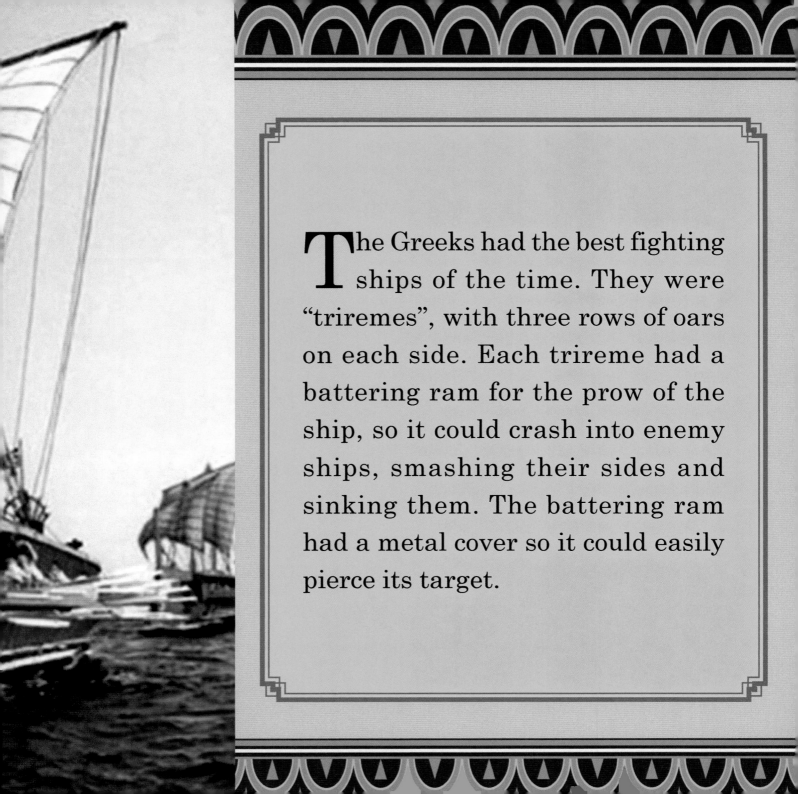

The Greeks had the best fighting ships of the time. They were "triremes", with three rows of oars on each side. Each trireme had a battering ram for the prow of the ship, so it could crash into enemy ships, smashing their sides and sinking them. The battering ram had a metal cover so it could easily pierce its target.

Themistocles, the leader of the Greek navy, brought his forces into the Strait of Salamis, where there was not much room to maneuver. The huge Persian fleet, with three ships for every Greek ship, clogged the strait.

Themistocles and a Human Sacrifice before Battle of Salamis

Xerxes I of Persia

In the fight, which the Persian King Xerxes watched from a throne on the shore as if it were a sports event, the Persians unwisely fell into the Greek trap by starting the battle in the strait, where there was not good room to maneuver. This was the same problem the army had faced at the pass of of Thermopylae. Persian ships crashed into other Persian ships, and the Persian fleet was not able to move to defend itself as the Greeks attacked. By the end of the day the Greeks had lost only forty ships while the Persians lost over 200.

This victory was the turning point in the war. The Greeks became confident that they could defeat the Persians whenever they needed to, and the Persians began to think about expanding their empire in other directions than Greece. If the Persians had won, they would probably have succeeded in adding Greece to their empire. Then the course of European and Near Eastern history might have been very different.

Greece

Athens

PLATAEA AND MYCALE

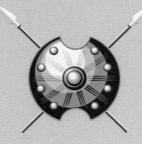

After Salamis, Xerxes returned to Persia. The Persian army, under a general called Mardonius, stayed northwest of Athens to try to continue conquering Greece. It was a huge force of over 300,000 men.

The allied Greek armies moved against this force, with Sparta in the lead. It was a much smaller force, but the Persians were reluctant to attack. They wanted to avoid any traps this time. After a while the Persian cavalry cut off the Greek supply lines. The Greeks decided to move back, and Mardonius thought they were running away. He ordered an attack. But the Greeks were ready to fight. Their long spears easily pierced the light shields of the Persians, and the Persians' short swords could not get past the Greeks' heavy shields.

Greek Warrior

Persian Warriors

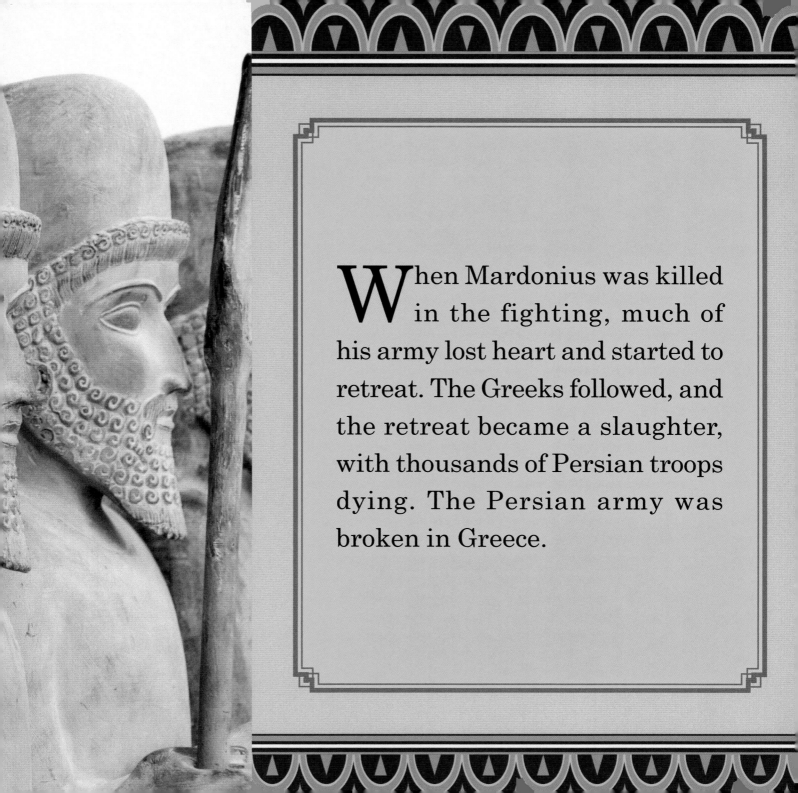

When Mardonius was killed in the fighting, much of his army lost heart and started to retreat. The Greeks followed, and the retreat became a slaughter, with thousands of Persian troops dying. The Persian army was broken in Greece.

On the same day, it is said, the Persian fleet was destroyed near Mycale on the Greek coast. The fleet wanted to avoid fighting the Greek navy, so they brought their ships to shore and tried to fight on land. It was not a great choice, and the Greeks had a convincing victory.

Mycale

Plain of Plataea

THIRTY MORE
YEARS OF WAR

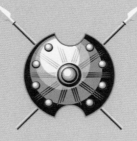

After the defeat at Plataea, and the disaster of
Mycale, the Persians lost interest in trying to
conquer Greece. The Greeks, however, went on the
offensive.

For the next thirty years Greek armies fought to free Greek city-states along the Turkish coast, with some success. But they could not complete the job because Persia had too large an army to defeat completely. Finally the two sides agreed on a peace treaty in 449 BCE.

Map of Persia

ANCIENT EMPIRES

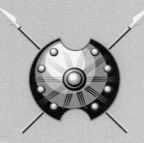

Greece not only defeated Persia in battle. Greek culture survived and was a model for the cultures of much of Europe and the Middle East even after the Persian Empire had collapsed.

Read more about ancient empires in the Baby Professor books Empress Wu: Breaking and Expanding China, The History of the Inca Empire, and Everything You Need to Know About the Rise and Fall of the Roman Empire In One Fat Book.

Ancient Inca City

Visit

BABY PROFESSOR
EDUCATION KIDS

www.BabyProfessorBooks.com

to download Free Baby Professor eBooks
and view our catalog of new and exciting
Children's Books

Made in the USA
Middletown, DE
22 June 2020